High Protein High Fiber Cookbook

40+ Beginner-Friendly Recipes With a Sample Meal Plan

copyright © 2025 Larry Jamesonn

All rights reserved No part of this book may be reproduced, or stored in a retrieval system, or transmitted in any form or by any means, electronic, mechanical, photocopying, recording, or otherwise, without express written permission of the publisher.

Disclaimer

By reading this disclaimer, you are accepting the terms of the disclaimer in full. If you disagree with this disclaimer, please do not read the guide.

All of the content within this guide is provided for informational and educational purposes only, and should not be accepted as independent medical or other professional advice. The author is not a doctor, physician, nurse, mental health provider, or registered nutritionist/dietician. Therefore, using and reading this guide does not establish any form of a physician-patient relationship.

Always consult with a physician or another qualified health provider with any issues or questions you might have regarding any sort of medical condition. Do not ever disregard any qualified professional medical advice or delay seeking that advice because of anything you have read in this guide. The information in this guide is not intended to be any sort of medical advice and should not be used in lieu of any medical advice by a licensed and qualified medical professional.

The information in this guide has been compiled from a variety of known sources. However, the author cannot attest to or guarantee the accuracy of each source and thus should not be held liable for any errors or omissions.

You acknowledge that the publisher of this guide will not be held liable for any loss or damage of any kind incurred as a result of this guide or the reliance on any information provided within this guide. You acknowledge and agree that you assume all risk and responsibility for any action you undertake in response to the information in this guide.

Using this guide does not guarantee any particular result (e.g., weight loss or a cure). By reading this guide, you acknowledge that there are no guarantees to any specific outcome or results you can expect.

All product names, diet plans, or names used in this guide are for identification purposes only and are the property of their respective owners. The use of these names does not imply endorsement. All other trademarks cited herein are the property of their respective owners.

Where applicable, this guide is not intended to be a substitute for the original work of this diet plan and is, at most, a supplement to the original work for this diet plan and never a direct substitute. This guide is a personal expression of the facts of that diet plan.

Where applicable, persons shown in the cover images are stock photography models and the publisher has obtained the rights to use the images through license agreements with third-party stock image companies.

Table of Contents

Introduction	**8**
Understanding High-Protein and High-Fiber Foods	**10**
High-Protein Foods	10
High-Fiber Foods	10
The Role of Protein and Fiber in the Body	11
Benefits of High Protein and High Fiber Diets	**13**
Improved Digestion and Gut Health	13
Enhanced Muscle Growth and Repair	13
Long-Lasting Energy and Satiety	14
Weight Management and Fat Loss	14
Better Blood Sugar Control	14
List of High-Protein and High-Fiber Foods	**16**
High Protein Foods	16
High Fiber Foods	18
5-Step Plan to Getting Started with High-Protein High-Fiber Foods	**20**
Step 1: Assess Your Current Diet	20
Step 2: Make a Shopping List	25
Step 3: Plan Your Meals	31
Step 4: Experiment with Recipes	36
Step 5: Stay Consistent	41
41 Beginner-Friendly and Quick Recipes	**48**
Overnight Oats with Chia Seeds and Berries	49
Scrambled Eggs with Spinach and Feta	51
Protein-Packed Smoothie with Greek Yogurt	53
Quinoa and Black Bean Salad	54
Grilled Chicken Wrap with Avocado and Spinach	56
Lentil Soup with Mixed Vegetables	58
Baked Salmon with Asparagus	60

Tofu Stir-Fry with Broccoli and Bell Peppers	61
Turkey Chili with Kidney Beans	63
Hummus with Carrot Sticks	65
Almond and Date Energy Balls	66
Greek Yogurt with Mixed Nuts	67
Avocado Toast with Whole Grain Bread	68
Cottage Cheese with Pineapple Chunks	69
Edamame with Sea Salt	70
Peanut Butter and Banana Rice Cakes	71
Cucumber Slices with Hummus	72
Turkey and Cheese Roll-Ups	73
Dark Chocolate and Almonds	74
Apple Slices with Almond Butter	75
Roasted Chickpeas with Spices	76
Hard-Boiled Eggs with Paprika	77
Berry and Nut Yogurt Parfait	78
Celery Sticks with Almond Butter	79
Mini Caprese Skewers	80
Popcorn with Nutritional Yeast	81
Quinoa Salad Cups	82
Smoked Salmon on Rye Crackers	83
Sweet Potato Chips with Guacamole	84
Trail Mix with Dried Fruit and Seeds	85
Carrot and Cucumber Sushi Rolls	86
Protein Pancakes with Berries	87
Chia Seed Pudding with Mango	89
Baked Kale Chips with Sea Salt	90
Zucchini Fries with Garlic Aioli	91
Pita Bread with Tzatziki Sauce	93
Lentil Dip with Veggie Sticks	94
Cheese and Cherry Tomato Bites	95

Banana Oat Bars	96
Egg Muffins with Spinach and Feta	97
Almond Butter and Chia Seed Toast	98
7-Day Sample Meal Plan	**99**
Day 1	99
Day 2	99
Day 3	100
Day 4	100
Day 5	100
Day 6	100
Day 7	101
Conclusion	**102**
FAQs	**105**
References and Helpful Links	**108**

Introduction

Achieving a nutritious diet requires understanding the key elements that contribute to overall wellness. Incorporating high-protein and high-fiber foods into your meals is essential for maintaining a balanced diet, as these foods provide vital nutrients for a healthier lifestyle. High-protein options like lean meats, fish, beans, and legumes support muscle development and repair, while high-fiber foods such as fruits, vegetables, and whole grains are important for digestive health and can help regulate blood sugar levels.

This combination enhances digestion, promotes muscle growth, and offers sustained energy, keeping you full longer and aiding in effective weight management. Embracing high-protein and high-fiber foods can transform your dietary habits and lead to lasting health benefits that improve your quality of life.

In this guide, we will talk about the following:

- Understanding High-Protein and High-Fiber Foods
- The Role of Protein and Fiber in the Body
- Benefits of High Protein and High Fiber Diets

- List of High-Protein and High-Fiber Foods
- 5-Step Plan To Getting Started with High-Protein High-Fiber Foods
- 41 Beginner-Friendly and Quick Recipes

Furthermore, a sample meal plan will offer you practical ideas on how to seamlessly integrate these nutritious foods into your daily routine, ensuring that you can easily maintain a balanced diet. Whether you're looking to boost your energy levels, manage your weight effectively, or simply adopt a healthier lifestyle, this guide will equip you with the knowledge, insights, and tools you need to succeed on your journey to better health. Keep reading to discover the power of high-protein and high-fiber foods and how they can positively impact your overall well-being.

Understanding High-Protein and High-Fiber Foods

To embark on a journey toward better health, it's essential to understand the building blocks of a nutritious diet: high protein and high fiber foods. These components not only fulfill our dietary needs but also enhance our overall well-being.

High-Protein Foods

High-protein foods are those rich in essential amino acids, the building blocks of proteins. These foods support the body's structural and functional demands. Common high-protein sources include meats, fish, eggs, dairy products, legumes, nuts, and seeds. Whether derived from animal or plant origins, these foods are crucial for maintaining muscle mass and fostering growth and repair.

High-Fiber Foods

High-fiber foods are those abundant in plant-based carbohydrates that the body cannot digest. Instead of being broken down into sugar, fiber passes through the body, aiding in various physiological processes. Fruits, vegetables, whole grains, legumes, and seeds are all excellent sources of fiber. Including these in your diet promotes digestive health and ensures a feeling of fullness.

The Role of Protein and Fiber in the Body

Protein's Role

Protein is vital for muscle repair and growth, making it indispensable for active individuals, athletes, and those recovering from injury. When you engage in physical activity, your muscles experience stress and tiny tears, and protein is essential for repairing this damage, allowing muscles to strengthen and grow over time.

Additionally, protein plays a crucial role in producing enzymes and hormones that regulate numerous bodily functions, from digestion to metabolism. It also helps maintain cell structure, ensuring that cells remain healthy and functional.

Protein is integral to supporting immune function, as it contributes to the production of antibodies that help defend the body against infections. By consuming enough high-quality protein through sources like lean meats, dairy, legumes, and nuts, you provide your body with the essential tools necessary for repair, development, and optimal overall functioning.

Fiber's Role

Fiber is a crucial component in promoting healthy digestion and maintaining gut health. It adds bulk to stool, which plays an important role in facilitating regular bowel movements and preventing constipation, a common issue that can lead to discomfort and other digestive problems. Fiber is instrumental in managing blood sugar levels by slowing the absorption of sugar into the bloodstream.

This mechanism not only helps prevent spikes and crashes in energy but also supports overall metabolic health. The gradual absorption of sugar contributes to sustained energy levels throughout the day, making it easier for individuals to stay focused and energized for their daily activities. Including a variety of fiber-rich foods, such as fruits, vegetables, whole grains, and legumes, in one's diet can significantly enhance digestive health and promote a sense of well-being.

Understanding these fundamental aspects of high protein and high fiber foods lays the groundwork for making informed dietary choices. By integrating these nutrients into your meals, you can foster a healthier lifestyle, enhance bodily functions, and enjoy the benefits of a balanced diet.

Benefits of High Protein and High Fiber Diets

Adopting a high protein and high fiber diet can significantly influence your health and well-being, providing a range of benefits that extend beyond basic nutrition.

Improved Digestion and Gut Health

Dietary fiber is key to ensuring a healthy digestive system. It increases stool bulk, aiding in regular bowel movements and preventing constipation. A fiber-rich diet supports a diverse and thriving microbiome, which is crucial for a healthy gut. This not only improves digestion but also enhances the body's ability to absorb nutrients effectively.

Enhanced Muscle Growth and Repair

Proteins serve as the fundamental components for constructing muscle tissue. Eating sufficient high-protein foods aids in muscle growth and repair, which is especially crucial for those involved in regular exercise or strength training. Protein helps repair the tiny muscle tears that occur during exercise, fostering stronger and more resilient muscles.

Long-Lasting Energy and Satiety

Both protein and fiber contribute to sustained energy levels throughout the day. Protein takes longer to digest, which helps maintain steady energy levels and reduces the likelihood of energy crashes. Fiber, on the other hand, slows the digestion of carbohydrates, providing a gradual release of energy. Together, they promote a sense of fullness, reducing hunger pangs and preventing overeating.

Weight Management and Fat Loss

A diet high in protein and fiber can be an effective tool for weight management and fat loss. Protein boosts metabolism and increases the number of calories burned at rest. It also aids in preserving lean muscle mass during weight loss. Fiber contributes to satiety, which can lead to reduced calorie intake. Together, they create a dietary framework that supports healthy weight management.

Better Blood Sugar Control

Fiber is essential in managing blood sugar levels by slowing down sugar absorption, which helps prevent sudden increases and drops in blood glucose. This steady release of sugar into the bloodstream helps maintain balanced energy levels and reduces the risk of developing insulin resistance or type 2 diabetes. Additionally, protein can help stabilize blood sugar levels by slowing the absorption of carbohydrates.

Incorporating high protein and high fiber foods into your daily meals helps harness these benefits, supporting a healthier lifestyle and improving overall quality of life.

List of High-Protein and High-Fiber Foods

Understanding which foods are rich in protein and fiber is crucial for building a balanced, nutritious diet. Here's a comprehensive list to guide you in incorporating these essential nutrients into your meals.

High Protein Foods

1. **Lean Meats:**
    - Chicken: A versatile protein source, great for grilling, baking, or sautéing.
    - Turkey: Leaner than beef, turkey is ideal for sandwiches, salads, and roasts.
    - Beef: Choose lean cuts like sirloin or tenderloin for a protein-rich meal.

2. **Fish and Seafood:**
    - Salmon: Packed with omega-3 fatty acids, perfect for grilling or baking.
    - Tuna: A convenient option for salads and sandwiches, high in protein and low in fat.

- Shrimp: Quick to cook and rich in protein, shrimp is excellent in stir-fries or pasta dishes.

3. **Eggs and Dairy:**
   - Eggs: A complete protein source, eggs can be boiled, scrambled, or poached.
   - Greek Yogurt: Offers more protein than regular yogurt, perfect for breakfast or snacks.
   - Cheese: Varieties like cottage cheese and ricotta are high in protein and calcium.

4. **Plant-Based Proteins:**
   - Tofu: A flexible soy ingredient that takes on flavors effectively, making it perfect for stir-fries and soups.
   - Tempeh: Nutty-flavored fermented soy, excellent for grilling or sautéing.
   - Lentils: Rich in protein and fiber, lentils are perfect for soups and salads.
   - Chickpeas: Versatile in dishes like hummus, salads, and stews.

5. **Nuts and Seeds:**
   - Almonds: High in protein and healthy fats, suitable for snacks or as a salad topping.
   - Chia Seeds: Packed with nutrients, they add a crunch to smoothies and yogurt.
   - Hemp Seeds: Rich in omega-3 and omega-6, ideal for smoothies and salads.

High Fiber Foods

1. **Whole Grains:**
   - Oats: Great for breakfast, oats provide fiber and keep you full longer.
   - Quinoa: A complete protein and high in fiber, excellent in salads or as a rice substitute.
   - Brown Rice: A nutritious alternative to white rice, providing fiber and energy.

2. **Vegetables:**
   - Broccoli: High in fiber and vitamins, suitable for steaming or roasting.
   - Brussels Sprouts: A fiber-rich vegetable, delicious when roasted or sautéed.
   - Carrots: Crunchy and sweet, carrots are perfect raw or cooked.

3. **Fruits:**
   - Apples: A convenient fruit high in fiber, ideal for snacks or desserts.
   - Pears: Rich in fiber and vitamins, delicious raw or baked.
   - Berries: Blueberries, raspberries, and strawberries are fiber-packed and antioxidant-rich.

4. **Legumes:**
   - Beans: Varieties like black beans and kidney beans are great for soups and stews.
   - Lentils: Offer a hearty addition to soups and salads, high in protein and fiber.
   - Peas: Sweet and nutritious, perfect in soups or as a side dish.

5. **Seeds:**
   - Flaxseeds: Rich in fiber and omega-3, ideal for adding to smoothies or baked goods.
   - Chia Seeds: Provide a good amount of fiber and add texture to dishes.

Incorporating a variety of these high-protein and high-fiber foods into your daily diet can help you achieve a balanced nutritional intake, promoting overall health and well-being.

5-Step Plan to Getting Started with High-Protein High-Fiber Foods

To get started with incorporating high-protein and high-fiber foods into your diet, here is a simple 5-step plan to follow:

Step 1: Assess Your Current Diet

To successfully incorporate more high-protein and high-fiber foods into your diet, begin by thoroughly understanding your current eating habits. Here's a structured approach to help you make informed changes:

1. **Keep a Food Diary**

    Documenting everything you eat and drink for at least a week provides a comprehensive view of your dietary patterns and is a vital first step in improving your diet. Here's how to effectively keep a food diary:

    - *Record Details*: Include all meals, snacks, and drinks consumed throughout the day. Be sure to note the portion sizes, meal times, and any additional ingredients or condiments used. This

level of detail helps create an accurate picture of your eating habits.
- *Use Technology*: Consider using apps like MyFitnessPal or Cronometer to track your intake digitally. These tools often come with nutritional databases that can automatically calculate your consumption of proteins, fibers, and other nutrients.
- *Be Honest and Consistent*: Record everything you eat, even if it's not part of your regular diet. This honesty is crucial for identifying true patterns and pinpointing areas that need improvement.
- *Review and Reflect*: At the end of the week, take time to review your diary. Look for trends such as frequent snacking or meals that are consistently low in protein or fiber. Reflecting on these insights is key to understanding your current dietary habits.

2. **Identify Current Protein and Fiber Sources**

Reviewing your food diary to recognize existing sources of protein and fiber helps you understand what you're already doing right. Here's how to identify these sources:

- *Highlight and Categorize*: Go through your diary and highlight meals or snacks that contain protein and fiber. Common sources include meats, fish, beans, nuts, whole grains, fruits, and vegetables. Categorize these items to see how varied your intake is.

- ***Recognize Patterns***: Identify which meals consistently include protein and fiber. For instance, you might notice that your lunches often include whole grain sandwiches or salads with nuts and seeds.
- **Celebrate Healthy Choices**: Acknowledge the healthy habits you already have in place. This recognition can boost your confidence and motivation to continue improving your diet.
- *Assess Quality*: Consider the quality of the protein and fiber sources. Opt for lean proteins like chicken or turkey, and choose whole grains over refined ones for better nutritional value.

3. **Spot Nutritional Gaps**

Identifying meals that lack protein and fiber is crucial for making effective dietary changes. Here's how to spot these gaps:

- *Analyze Each Meal*: Look closely at each meal and snack in your diary. Breakfasts with sugary cereals or pastries, lunches with refined grains, or dinners without vegetables are common gaps.

- ***Identify Key Areas for Improvement***: Note any meals that regularly lack protein or fiber. For example, if your lunches often consist of white bread sandwiches, consider adding whole grain bread or a side of legumes.
- ***Prioritize Changes***: Focus on the meals with the most significant gaps first. Tackling one meal at a time can make dietary adjustments feel less daunting.
- ***Seek Balanced Options***: Strive for balanced meals that incorporate a source of protein, a high-fiber carbohydrate, and a serving of vegetables or fruits.

4. **Make Simple Swaps**

Small, manageable changes can have a significant impact on your diet. Here's how to make simple swaps:

- ***Identify Processed Foods***: Start by identifying processed snacks like chips and cookies in your diet. These can be replaced with healthier alternatives.
- ***Choose High-Fiber Alternatives***: Opt for fresh fruits such as apples or berries, which are high in fiber, as snacks. These not only satisfy sweet cravings but also provide essential nutrients.

- ***Incorporate Legumes***: Add legumes like lentils or chickpeas to salads and soups. They are excellent sources of protein and fiber and can easily enhance the nutritional value of your meals.
- ***Experiment with Whole Grains***: Swap refined grains with whole grains such as brown rice, quinoa, or whole wheat pasta to increase fiber intake.

5. **Gradual Changes for Sustainability**

Adopting gradual changes is essential for long-term success. Here's how to make sustainable adjustments:

- ***Introduce Changes Slowly***: Aim to introduce one new high-protein or high-fiber food each week. This gradual approach allows your body and palate to adjust without feeling overwhelmed.
- ***Focus on Consistency***: Build a routine that includes these new foods regularly. This consistency helps transform changes into lasting habits.
- ***Monitor Your Adaptation***: Pay attention to how your body responds to dietary changes. Adjust portion sizes or food choices as needed to maintain comfort and satisfaction.

- ***Stay Patient***: Remember that significant results take time. Patience and persistence are vital as you work towards a healthier diet that you can sustain long-term.

By carefully assessing your current diet and making thoughtful changes, you can seamlessly transition to a more nutritious, protein-rich, and fiber-filled eating plan.

Step 2: Make a Shopping List

Creating a shopping list is a crucial step in incorporating more high-protein and high-fiber foods into your diet. A well-organized list helps you stay focused while shopping and ensures you have all the ingredients needed for nutritious meals. Here's how to craft an effective shopping list:

1. **Review Your Dietary Goals**

    Reflecting on your dietary goals is a crucial step in improving your eating habits and ensuring you meet your nutritional needs. Here's how to effectively review and align with your dietary goals:

    - ***Analyze Improvement Areas***: Use your dietary assessment to pinpoint areas that need enhancement. This might include increasing protein intake or incorporating more fiber-rich foods.

- ***Select Beneficial Foods***: Decide which high-protein and high-fiber foods will be most beneficial for your meals. Consider foods that align with your health objectives, such as lean meats for muscle building or fiber-rich fruits for improved digestion.
- ***Set Priorities***: Prioritize foods that address your most pressing dietary needs. This focus will guide your grocery selections and ensure you're targeting the most critical areas for improvement.
- ***Visualize Success***: Picture the benefits of achieving your dietary goals, such as increased energy levels or improved overall health. This visualization can motivate you to choose foods that support your objectives.

2. **Categorize Your List**

Organizing your grocery list by category can streamline shopping and ensure a balanced diet. Here's how to categorize effectively:

- ***Divide by Food Groups***: Break your list into categories such as proteins, fibers, fruits, vegetables, grains, and snacks. This structure simplifies shopping and ensures all essential groups are covered.

- *Use Subcategories*: For larger categories, create subcategories. For instance, under proteins, include lean meats, fish, and plant-based options like beans and tofu.
- *Prioritize Essentials*: Highlight must-have items within each category to ensure you don't overlook key ingredients.
- *Utilize a Template*: Consider using a pre-made list template or app that organizes by categories automatically, saving time and effort.

3. Proteins

Incorporating a variety of protein sources into your diet is essential for muscle maintenance and overall health. Here's how to enhance your protein intake:

- *Lean Meats*: Opt for chicken and turkey, which are lower in fat and high in protein. These meats are versatile and can be used in a variety of dishes.
- *Fish Choices*: Include omega-3-rich fish like salmon and tuna, which support heart health alongside being excellent protein sources.
- *Plant-Based Proteins*: Beans, lentils, chickpeas, and tofu provide protein and fiber, making them excellent choices for vegetarians or those looking to reduce meat intake.

- **Eggs**: A highly versatile protein source, eggs can be included in breakfasts, salads, and snacks.

4. **Fibers**

   Boosting your fiber intake is key for digestive health and satiety. Here's how to choose high-fiber foods:

   - **Fruits**: Select fruits like apples, pears, and berries, which are high in fiber and antioxidants.
   - **Vegetables**: Incorporate fiber-rich vegetables such as broccoli, spinach, and carrots into meals to enhance nutritional value.
   - **Whole Grains**: Opt for whole grains like quinoa, oats, and brown rice over refined grains to increase fiber content in your diet.
   - **Incorporate Variety**: Rotate different fruits and vegetables to cover a broad spectrum of nutrients and keep meals exciting.

5. **Plan for Variety**

   Variety in your diet helps prevent monotony and ensures a well-rounded nutrient intake. Here's how to plan for variety:

   - **Mix Protein Sources**: To keep your meals interesting and nutritious, rotate between various protein sources each week. For example, one week you could enjoy grilled chicken, while the next week you might swap it for flavorful fish or plant-based tofu. This variety not only enhances taste but also ensures you receive a diverse range of nutrients.

- *Seasonal Ingredients*: Incorporate seasonal produce into your meals whenever possible. Seasonal fruits and vegetables are often fresher, tastier, and more budget-friendly, making them a great choice for enhancing your dishes. Plus, using local ingredients supports nearby farmers and reduces your carbon footprint.
- *Experiment with Recipes*: Don't be afraid to step out of your culinary comfort zone! Trying new recipes can challenge your usual cooking routine and introduce you to exciting flavor profiles and unfamiliar ingredients. Whether it's a spicy curry or a refreshing salad, experimenting can make cooking more enjoyable and broaden your palate.
- *Balanced Meals*: Strive for meals that achieve a balance of protein, fiber, and healthy fats across different food groups. This approach not only helps keep you satiated but also ensures you're getting a well-rounded nutritional profile. Consider including lean meats, whole grains, legumes, fruits, and vegetables to create meals

that nourish your body and satisfy your taste buds.

6. Consider Meal Prep Needs

Planning for meal prep can save time and keep you on track with your dietary goals. Here's how to consider meal prep needs:

- *Plan Weekly Menus*: Outline meals for the week, ensuring you have all the necessary ingredients.
- *Batch Cooking*: Cook in batches to save time on busy days, storing meals in portion-sized containers for easy access.
- *Prep Ingredients*: Pre-chop vegetables or marinate proteins ahead of time to streamline cooking during the week.
- *Adapt to Your Schedule*: Adjust meal prep based on your weekly commitments, ensuring it remains practical and manageable.

7. Stay Flexible and Budget-Friendly

Maintaining flexibility and being budget-conscious are essential for a sustainable diet. Here's how to stay adaptable:

- *Swap Based on Availability*: Be open to swapping items based on what's in season or on sale to save money.

- **Bulk Purchases**: Consider buying non-perishable high-protein or high-fiber foods in bulk for cost savings.
- **Try New Foods**: Use sales as an opportunity to try new foods that align with your dietary goals, possibly discovering new favorites.
- **Budget Planning**: Allocate a specific budget for groceries and stick to it by planning meals around affordable yet nutritious items.

By following these structured steps, you can create a successful plan that supports your dietary goals and leads to a healthier lifestyle.

By planning ahead and creating a comprehensive shopping list, you can streamline your grocery trips and ensure that you always have the necessary ingredients for nutritious, protein-rich, and fiber-filled meals. This approach not only saves time and reduces stress but also keeps you committed to your dietary improvements.

Step 3: Plan Your Meals

Meal planning is an effective strategy to incorporate high-protein and high-fiber foods into your diet consistently. By using your shopping list as a guide, you can streamline your weekly meal preparation and enjoy numerous benefits. Here's how to plan your meals efficiently:

1. **Set a Weekly Meal Schedule**

   Creating a weekly meal schedule is a foundational step in maintaining a balanced and nutritious diet. Here's how to effectively plan your meals:

   - *Outline the Week*: Begin by mapping out breakfast, lunch, dinner, and snacks for each day. Use your shopping list to ensure that your meals incorporate the high-protein and high-fiber foods you've selected.
   - *Balance Nutrients*: Distribute protein and fiber sources evenly across your meals. For example, plan to include a protein-rich breakfast like eggs and whole grain toast, a fiber-packed lunch with a legume salad, and a balanced dinner with lean meat and vegetables.
   - *Consider Your Schedule*: Align your meals with your daily routine. Plan quicker meals on busier days and more elaborate ones when you have extra time.
   - *Visual Calendar*: Use a digital calendar or a handwritten planner to visualize your meal plan. This clarity helps keep you organized and on track.

2. **Incorporate Variety**

   Variety is key to a nutritionally balanced diet and helps prevent meal fatigue. Here's how to add diversity to your meals:

   - *Mix Protein Sources*: Rotate between different protein options like poultry, fish, legumes, and plant-based proteins to cover a wide range of nutrients.
   - *Seasonal Selections*: Choose seasonal fruits and vegetables, which are often more flavorful and nutrient-rich.
   - *Culinary Exploration*: Experiment with cuisines from around the world, trying dishes like Asian stir-fries, Mediterranean salads, or Mexican-inspired bowls.
   - *Colorful Plates*: Aim for a rainbow of colors on your plate, indicating a variety of nutrients. Incorporate different textures and flavors to keep meals exciting.

3. **Batch Cooking and Prep**

   Batch cooking and preparing ingredients ahead of time can significantly reduce the stress of daily meal preparation. Here's how to streamline your cooking process:

- ***Designate a Day***: Choose a day for batch cooking—often Sunday works well—to prepare staples like grains, beans, or roasted vegetables.
- ***Cook in Bulk***: Prepare large quantities of versatile ingredients that can be used in multiple meals, such as quinoa, brown rice, or grilled chicken.
- ***Pre-Chop Ingredients***: Wash and chop vegetables in advance. Store them in airtight containers for easy access throughout the week.
- ***Freezer-Friendly Meals***: Consider making extra portions to freeze for later use, especially for soups, stews, or casseroles.

4. **Portion Control and Storage**

Proper portion control and storage are essential for maintaining a healthy diet and avoiding food waste. Here's how to manage portions effectively:

- ***Plan Portions***: Use measuring tools or visual cues to portion out meals. For example, a protein portion should be about the size of your palm.
- ***Pre-Portion Meals***: Store meals in individual containers to prevent overeating and make it easy to grab a balanced meal on the go.

- ***Label Containers***: Label meals with the date and contents to keep track of freshness and avoid spoilage.
- ***Smart Storage***: Use clear containers to easily see the contents, encouraging consumption before spoilage.

5. **Opt for Simple Recipes**

Simple recipes can align with your dietary goals without overwhelming your schedule. Here's how to choose and prepare them:

- ***Easy Ingredients***: Select recipes that require minimal ingredients and are versatile, like stir-fries or sheet pan dinners.
- ***Quick Cooking Methods***: Utilize methods such as grilling, roasting, or steaming, which are efficient and preserve nutrients.
- ***Breakfast Simplicity***: Try overnight oats with nuts and fruit for a quick, nutritious breakfast.
- ***Dinner Efficiency***: Go for one-pot meals or salads that combine protein, greens, and grains for a balanced dinner.

6. **Adjust and Adapt**

Flexibility is crucial for maintaining enthusiasm and adherence to your meal plan. Here's how to stay adaptable:

- *Seasonal Swaps*: Replace ingredients with seasonal or sale items to keep costs down and flavors fresh.
- *Meal Swapping*: If you're not in the mood for a planned meal, switch it to another one scheduled for the week.
- *Innovate Leftovers*: Use leftovers creatively, perhaps turning roasted vegetables into a frittata or adding grilled chicken to a salad.
- *Stay Open*: Be willing to try new foods and recipes, adjusting your plan based on new discoveries or changing preferences.

By following these steps, you can maintain a balanced, nutritious diet that is both enjoyable and sustainable, helping you achieve your dietary goals effectively.

By planning your meals around high-protein and high-fiber foods, you establish a routine that supports your health goals. Meal planning not only helps you maintain consistency in your diet but also saves time and reduces food waste, ultimately leading to financial savings. This strategic approach empowers you to stick to your healthy eating plan with ease and enjoyment.

Step 4: Experiment with Recipes

Exploring new recipes is a fantastic way to incorporate high-protein and high-fiber foods into your meals, keeping your diet both exciting and nutritious. Here's how to dive into culinary experimentation effectively:

1. **Seek Out New Recipes**

   Exploring new recipes is a great way to diversify your meals and introduce high-protein and high-fiber foods into your diet. Here's how to effectively seek out new recipe ideas:

   - *Online Resources*: Begin with popular websites like Cooking Light, Epicurious, and EatingWell, which offer an array of recipes tailored to different dietary needs, including high-protein and high-fiber options.
   - *Cookbooks*: Invest in cookbooks focused on healthy eating, such as "The High-Protein Vegetarian Cookbook" or "The Fiber Effect." These books provide curated recipes that can inspire your meal planning.
   - *Food Blogs*: Explore food blogs that specialize in healthy recipes. These blogs often include personal anecdotes and tips that can enhance your cooking experience.
   - *Recipe Apps*: Utilize recipe apps that allow you to search for dishes based on dietary preferences, making it easier to find suitable meals.

2. Embrace Different Cuisines

Incorporating global cuisines can naturally increase your intake of high-protein and high-fiber foods. Here's how to embrace culinary diversity:

- *Mediterranean Cuisine*: Try dishes that feature legumes, grains, and fish. Mediterranean diets are known for their health benefits and flavorful ingredients.
- *Indian Cuisine*: Explore the rich variety of Indian dishes that use lentils, chickpeas, and spices to create hearty, protein-rich meals.
- *Asian Cuisine*: Experiment with Asian stir-fries or sushi that incorporate tofu, edamame, or quinoa for a nutritious twist.
- *Latin American Cuisine*: Enjoy Latin American dishes that include beans, quinoa, and avocados, known for their high fiber content.

3. Test New Cooking Methods

Experimenting with different cooking methods can enhance flavors and textures in your meals. Here's how to incorporate various techniques:

- *Grilling*: Grilling can add a smoky flavor to meats and vegetables, making them more appealing and tasty.

- ***Roasting***: Roasting vegetables or chickpeas can bring out their natural sweetness and provide a crispy texture, making them a delicious snack.
- ***Steaming***: Preserve nutrients in vegetables by steaming them, a method that maintains their vibrant colors and crunch.
- ***Stir-Frying***: Quickly cook meats and vegetables while preserving their nutrients with stir-frying, which requires minimal oil.

4. **Adapt and Modify**

Customizing recipes to fit your dietary needs or taste preferences is crucial for a sustainable diet. Here's how to adapt and modify effectively:

- ***Ingredient Substitution***: Swap ingredients to enhance nutritional value, like using quinoa instead of rice for extra protein.
- ***Healthier Alternatives***: Replace high-calorie components with healthier options, such as using Greek yogurt in place of sour cream.
- ***Flavor Adjustments***: Modify seasonings and spices to suit your taste while maintaining the dish's nutritional integrity.
- ***Allergy Considerations***: Ensure you adjust recipes to accommodate any food allergies or sensitivities, ensuring everyone can enjoy the meal.

5. **Engage with Cooking Communities**

   Connecting with cooking communities can provide support and inspiration. Here's how to engage with these groups:

   - *Online Forums*: Participate in forums like Reddit's r/HealthyFood where members share recipes and cooking tips.
   - *Social Media Groups*: Join Facebook groups or Instagram communities focused on healthy eating where you can exchange ideas and seek advice.
   - *Cooking Classes*: Attend local or online cooking classes to learn new techniques and meet fellow cooking enthusiasts.
   - *Recipe Sharing*: Contribute your own recipes and modifications to these communities, fostering a sense of belonging and collaboration.

6. **Maintain a Recipe Journal**

   Keeping a recipe journal helps track your culinary journey and improvements. Here's how to maintain one:

   - *Document Recipes*: Write down recipes you've tried, including any adjustments you made and the results.

- ***Rate Your Dishes***: Note which dishes were particularly successful and which ones need tweaking, helping you refine your favorites.
- ***Personalized Cookbook***: Over time, your journal will serve as a personal cookbook tailored to your tastes and dietary goals.
- ***Reflect and Revise***: Regularly revisit and update your journal, allowing you to reflect on your progress and continuously refine your cooking skills.

By following these steps, you can enhance your culinary skills, enjoy diverse and nutritious meals, and maintain a healthy diet.

By experimenting with recipes, you introduce creativity and diversity into your diet, making healthy eating more enjoyable and sustainable. This approach not only enhances your culinary skills but also prevents meal monotony, encouraging you to maintain a balanced diet rich in protein and fiber.

Step 5: Stay Consistent

Consistency is key when it comes to reaping the benefits of a high-protein and high-fiber diet. Transitioning your eating habits requires patience and dedication, but maintaining these changes will lead to long-term health benefits. Here's how to stay consistent:

1. **Set Realistic Goals**

   Starting with realistic and achievable goals is crucial for long-term success in improving your diet. Here's how to set effective dietary goals:

   - *Small Steps*: Begin by incorporating one high-protein or high-fiber food into each meal. For example, add a serving of beans to your salad or swap white bread for whole-grain options.
   - *Weekly Challenges*: Challenge yourself to try a new recipe each week. This keeps your meal plan fresh and allows you to gradually build a repertoire of healthy dishes.
   - *Lifestyle Alignment*: Consider your current lifestyle and schedule. Opt for goals that are manageable, such as preparing home-cooked meals three times a week if you're often short on time.
   - *Gradual Adjustments*: Focus on making incremental changes rather than overhauling your diet overnight. This approach reduces the risk of feeling overwhelmed and increases the likelihood of success.

2. **Track Your Progress**

   Monitoring your dietary intake is essential for accountability and improvement. Here's how to effectively track your progress:

   - *Food Diary*: Keep a detailed food diary noting what you eat, portion sizes, and meal times. This helps identify patterns and areas needing adjustment.
   - *Nutrition Apps*: Use apps like MyFitnessPal or Cronometer to track your daily consumption of protein and fiber. These tools provide visual insights into your dietary habits.
   - *Celebrate Milestones*: Recognize and celebrate small victories, such as consistently meeting your daily fiber intake goal. This positive reinforcement keeps motivation high.
   - *Reflect Regularly*: Periodically review your progress to assess what's working and what might need change, allowing for continual improvement.

3. **Build a Routine**

   Creating a consistent routine helps turn new dietary habits into lasting practices. Here's how to establish a routine effectively:

- *Meal Planning*: Dedicate time each week to plan your meals. Consider designating specific days for grocery shopping and meal prep to ensure you have healthy options readily available.
- *Consistency*: Try to eat meals at the same times each day. This not only helps with digestion but also helps prevent mindless snacking.
- *Preparation*: Keep your kitchen stocked with staples like whole grains, nuts, and fresh produce, making it easier to prepare nutritious meals.
- *Automate Choices*: Simplify decisions by having a go-to list of healthy snacks or meal options, reducing the temptation to opt for less healthy choices when you're busy.

4. **Adapt to Challenges**

Anticipating and overcoming challenges is crucial to maintaining your dietary goals. Here's how to adapt to potential obstacles:

- *Busy Schedules*: Prepare snacks like mixed nuts or fruit in advance for busy days to ensure you have healthy options on hand.
- *Social Events*: When dining out, review restaurant menus in advance to choose meals that align with your dietary goals.

- *Flexibility*: Be open to adjusting your meal plan if unexpected events arise. Adaptability ensures you stay on track without feeling deprived.
- *Problem-Solving*: Identify common barriers you face and brainstorm solutions ahead of time, such as batch cooking on weekends to ease weekly meal preparation.

5. **Seek Support**

   Having a support system can significantly enhance your commitment to dietary changes. Here's how to find and utilize support:

   - *Share Goals*: Inform friends and family about your dietary goals. Their encouragement can provide motivation and accountability.
   - *Join Communities*: Engage with online or local communities focused on nutrition and healthy living, where members share tips and experiences.
   - *Buddy System*: Partner with someone who shares similar goals. You can support each other in staying committed and celebrating achievements together.
   - *Professional Guidance*: Consider consulting a nutritionist or dietitian for personalized advice and support in reaching your dietary objectives.

6. **Focus on Long-Term Benefits**

   Understanding the long-term benefits of your dietary changes can help maintain motivation. Here's how to keep the big picture in mind:

   - *Health Improvements*: Remember that a high-protein and high-fiber diet can improve digestion, energy levels, and overall health over time.
   - *Sustained Energy*: Focus on the increased energy levels and improved mood that come with a balanced diet, which can enhance daily life.
   - *Disease Prevention*: Keep in mind the role of diet in preventing chronic diseases, such as heart disease or diabetes, as a powerful motivator.
   - *Visual Reminders*: Use visual aids, like vision boards or affirmations, to remind yourself of the long-term benefits you're working toward.

7. **Be Patient and Persistent**

   Patience and persistence are key to achieving dietary success. Here's how to maintain them:

   - *Realistic Expectations*: Recognize that changes in diet and health take time. Avoid expecting immediate results to prevent discouragement.

- ***Learning from Setbacks***: View setbacks as learning opportunities. Analyze what went wrong and adjust your approach accordingly.
- ***Consistency Over Perfection***: Focus on being consistent rather than perfect. It's normal to have days that don't go as planned, but persistence will lead to success.
- ***Long-Term Vision***: Keep your long-term health goals in mind, and remind yourself that persistence will ultimately lead to the desired results.

By following this 5-step plan, you can easily get started with incorporating more high-protein and high-fiber foods into your diet. Not only will this help with weight management, but it can also promote overall health and well-being by providing your body with essential nutrients that are necessary for optimal functioning. Remember to listen to your body's needs and make adjustments as needed, but always strive to maintain a balanced nutritional intake for a healthier lifestyle.

41 Beginner-Friendly and Quick Recipes

Now that we have covered the basics of a high protein and high fiber diet, let's put it into practice with some delicious and easy recipes. Whether you're new to cooking or just looking for quick meal ideas, these beginner-friendly recipes are perfect for incorporating high-protein and high-fiber foods into your meals.

Overnight Oats with Chia Seeds and Berries

Ingredients:

- 1/2 cup rolled oats
- 1 tablespoon chia seeds
- 1 cup almond milk (or any milk of your choice)
- 1/2 teaspoon vanilla extract
- 1 tablespoon honey or maple syrup (optional)
- 1/2 cup mixed berries (strawberries, blueberries, raspberries)
- A pinch of salt

Instructions:

1. In a mason jar or a bowl, combine oats, chia seeds, and a pinch of salt.
2. Add almond milk and vanilla extract to the dry ingredients and stir well to ensure the chia seeds are evenly distributed.
3. Sweeten with honey or maple syrup if desired. Mix again.
4. Cover and refrigerate overnight or for at least 4 hours to allow the oats and chia seeds to soak and thicken.
5. Before serving, give the oats a good stir, then top with mixed berries.

6. Enjoy cold, or heat quickly in the microwave if a warm breakfast is preferred.

Tip: To enhance the nutritional value, consider adding a tablespoon of your favorite nut butter or a sprinkle of nuts for extra protein and crunch.

Scrambled Eggs with Spinach and Feta

Ingredients:

- 3 large eggs
- 1 cup fresh spinach, roughly chopped
- 1/4 cup feta cheese, crumbled
- 1 tablespoon olive oil or butter
- Salt and pepper to taste

Instructions:

1. Crack the eggs into a bowl, season with salt and pepper, and whisk until the yolks and whites are fully combined.
2. In a non-stick skillet, heat olive oil or butter over medium heat.
3. Add the chopped spinach and sauté for 1-2 minutes until wilted.
4. Pour the eggs over the spinach and let them sit, undisturbed, for about 30 seconds.
5. Gently stir the eggs with a spatula, lifting and folding them over from the edges to the center until they start to set.
6. Sprinkle in the feta cheese and continue to gently fold the eggs until they are cooked to your liking.

7. Serve immediately, and enjoy the creamy texture with a side of whole-grain toast.

Tip: For added flavor, toss in some diced tomatoes or a pinch of dried herbs like oregano or basil.

Protein-Packed Smoothie with Greek Yogurt

Ingredients:

- 1 cup Greek yogurt
- 1 banana, sliced
- 1/2 cup frozen berries
- 1 tablespoon almond butter
- 1 tablespoon chia seeds
- 1 cup almond milk (or any milk of your choice)
- A handful of spinach (optional for extra nutrients)

Instructions:

1. In a blender, combine Greek yogurt, banana, frozen berries, and almond butter.
2. Add chia seeds and almond milk to the blender.
3. For an extra nutritional boost, add a handful of spinach.
4. Blend on high until smooth and creamy.
5. Pour into a glass and enjoy immediately.

Tip: Adjust the consistency by adding more almond milk if you prefer a thinner smoothie. You can also add a scoop of your favorite protein powder for an even higher protein content.

Quinoa and Black Bean Salad

Ingredients:

- 1 cup quinoa
- 1 can (15 oz) black beans, drained and rinsed
- 1 cup cherry tomatoes, halved
- 1 red bell pepper, diced
- 1/4 cup red onion, finely chopped
- 1/4 cup fresh cilantro, chopped
- 2 tablespoons olive oil
- Juice of 1 lime
- Salt and pepper to taste

Instructions:

1. Rinse quinoa under cold water. Cook according to package instructions (usually 2 cups of water per 1 cup of quinoa), then let it cool.
2. In a large bowl, combine cooked quinoa, black beans, cherry tomatoes, red bell pepper, red onion, and cilantro.
3. In a small bowl, whisk together olive oil, lime juice, salt, and pepper.
4. Pour the dressing over the quinoa mixture and toss to combine.

5. Adjust seasoning to taste and serve chilled or at room temperature.

Tip: For extra flavor, add a diced avocado or a sprinkle of feta cheese before serving.

Grilled Chicken Wrap with Avocado and Spinach

Ingredients:

- 2 boneless, skinless chicken breasts
- 1 tablespoon olive oil
- 1 teaspoon garlic powder
- Salt and pepper to taste
- 4 whole-grain tortillas
- 1 avocado, sliced
- 1 cup fresh spinach leaves
- 1/4 cup Greek yogurt
- 1 tablespoon lemon juice

Instructions:

1. Preheat the grill to medium-high heat. Season chicken breasts with olive oil, garlic powder, salt, and pepper.
2. Grill chicken for 6-7 minutes on each side or until fully cooked. Remove from grill and let rest for a few minutes, then slice into strips.
3. In a small bowl, mix Greek yogurt and lemon juice to make a simple sauce.
4. Lay out tortillas and spread a spoonful of the yogurt sauce on each.

5. Layer with spinach, avocado slices, and grilled chicken.
6. Roll up the tortillas tightly, cut in half, and serve.

Tip: For added flavor, include sliced red onion or a sprinkle of your favorite cheese inside the wrap.

Lentil Soup with Mixed Vegetables

Ingredients:

- One cup of lentils, rinsed
- Two tablespoons of olive oil
- One onion, chopped
- Two carrots, diced
- Two celery stalks, diced
- Three cloves of garlic, minced
- One can of diced tomatoes (14.5 oz)
- Six cups of vegetable broth
- One teaspoon of cumin
- One teaspoon of thyme
- Salt and pepper to taste
- Two cups of chopped spinach or kale

Instructions:

1. In a large pot, warm up the olive oil on medium heat. Add onion, carrots, and celery, and sauté for 5-7 minutes until softened.
2. Stir in garlic, cumin, and thyme, and cook for another minute.
3. Add lentils, diced tomatoes, and vegetable broth to the pot. Bring to a boil, then reduce heat to a simmer.
4. Cook for 25-30 minutes or until lentils are tender.

5. Stir in spinach or kale and cook for an additional 5 minutes until wilted.
6. Season with salt and pepper to taste and serve hot.

Tip: For a heartier soup, add diced potatoes or sweet potatoes when adding the lentils.

Baked Salmon with Asparagus

Ingredients:

- Four salmon fillets
- One bundle of asparagus, trimmed at the ends
- Two tablespoons of olive oil
- Two tablespoons of lemon juice, freshly squeezed
- Two cloves of garlic, minced
- Salt and pepper, for seasoning
- Lemon slices for garnish

Instructions:

1. Preheat the oven to 400°F (200°C).
2. In a small bowl, mix olive oil, lemon juice, garlic, salt, and pepper.
3. Place salmon fillets and asparagus on a baking sheet lined with parchment paper.
4. Drizzle the olive oil mixture over the salmon and asparagus. Toss the asparagus lightly to coat.
5. Bake for 12-15 minutes, or until the salmon is cooked through and flaky.
6. Garnish with lemon slices and serve immediately.

Tip: For added flavor, sprinkle chopped fresh dill or parsley over the salmon before serving.

Tofu Stir-Fry with Broccoli and Bell Peppers

Ingredients:

- 1 block of firm tofu, pressed and cubed
- 2 tablespoons soy sauce
- 1 tablespoon sesame oil
- 2 tablespoons vegetable oil
- 2 cups broccoli florets
- 1 red bell pepper, sliced
- 1 yellow bell pepper, sliced
- 2 cloves garlic, minced
- 1 tablespoon fresh ginger, minced
- 2 tablespoons hoisin sauce

Instructions:

1. In a bowl, marinate tofu cubes with soy sauce and sesame oil for about 15 minutes.
2. Heat vegetable oil in a large skillet or wok over medium-high heat.
3. Add tofu cubes and cook until golden brown on all sides. Remove from the skillet and set aside.
4. In the same skillet, add garlic and ginger, sauté for 1 minute until fragrant.
5. Add broccoli and bell peppers, and stir-fry for 5-6 minutes until the vegetables are crisp-tender.

6. Return the tofu to the skillet, add hoisin sauce, and toss everything to combine. Cook for an additional 2 minutes.
7. Serve hot, optionally with steamed rice or quinoa.

Tip: Add sesame seeds or chopped scallions for extra texture and flavor.

Turkey Chili with Kidney Beans

Ingredients:

- One pound of ground turkey
- One tablespoon of olive oil
- One onion, chopped
- Two cloves of garlic, minced
- One red bell pepper, diced
- Two cans of kidney beans (15 oz each), drained and rinsed
- One can of diced tomatoes (28 oz)
- Two tablespoons of chili powder
- One teaspoon of cumin
- Salt and pepper to taste
- Optional toppings: shredded cheese, sour cream, chopped cilantro

Instructions:

1. In a sizable pot, warm the olive oil over medium heat. Incorporate the onion and garlic, cooking them until they become tender.
2. Incorporate the ground turkey into the pot, cooking it until it is browned and fully cooked, while breaking it apart with a spoon.
3. Stir in diced bell pepper, kidney beans, diced tomatoes, chili powder, and cumin. Mix well.

4. Bring to a boil, then reduce heat to low and let simmer for 30-40 minutes, stirring occasionally.
5. Season with salt and pepper to taste.
6. Serve hot, topped with shredded cheese, sour cream, or chopped cilantro if desired.

Tip: For extra heat, add a pinch of cayenne pepper or diced jalapeños to the chili.

Hummus with Carrot Sticks

Ingredients:

- 1 can (15 oz) chickpeas, drained and rinsed
- 1/4 cup tahini
- 2 tablespoons olive oil
- 2 tablespoons lemon juice
- 2 cloves garlic, minced
- 1/2 teaspoon ground cumin
- Salt to taste
- Water (as needed for consistency)
- 4-5 large carrots, peeled and cut into sticks

Instructions:

1. In a food processor, combine chickpeas, tahini, olive oil, lemon juice, garlic, cumin, and salt.
2. Blend until smooth, adding water a tablespoon at a time to achieve the desired consistency.
3. Transfer the hummus to a serving bowl and drizzle with olive oil for extra flavor.
4. Serve with carrot sticks for dipping.

Tip: For a spicy kick, add a pinch of cayenne pepper or smoked paprika to the hummus.

Almond and Date Energy Balls

Ingredients:

- 1 cup almonds
- 1 cup pitted dates
- 1 tablespoon chia seeds
- 1 tablespoon cocoa powder
- 1 teaspoon vanilla extract
- A pinch of salt

Instructions:

1. In a food processor, pulse almonds until finely chopped.
2. Add dates, chia seeds, cocoa powder, vanilla extract, and salt. Process until the mixture is well combined and sticky.
3. Roll the mixture into small balls, about one inch in diameter.
4. Place the energy balls on a plate and refrigerate for at least 30 minutes to firm up.

Tip: Roll the energy balls in shredded coconut or crushed nuts for added texture and flavor.

Greek Yogurt with Mixed Nuts

Ingredients:

- 1 cup Greek yogurt
- 1/4 cup mixed nuts (almonds, walnuts, pecans)
- 1 tablespoon honey
- 1/2 teaspoon cinnamon
- Optional: fresh berries or a sprinkle of granola

Instructions:

1. In a serving bowl, place Greek yogurt and smooth the top.
2. Drizzle honey over the yogurt and sprinkle with cinnamon.
3. Top with mixed nuts, distributing them evenly.
4. Add fresh berries or granola if desired for extra flavor and crunch.

Tip: Toast the nuts lightly in a dry skillet over medium heat for enhanced flavor before adding them to the yogurt.

Avocado Toast with Whole Grain Bread

Ingredients:

- 1 ripe avocado
- 2 slices of whole-grain bread
- 1/4 teaspoon salt
- 1/4 teaspoon black pepper
- 1 tablespoon lemon juice
- Optional: 2 poached eggs

Instructions:

1. Toast the slices of whole grain bread until golden and crisp.
2. Cut the avocado in half, remove the pit, and scoop the flesh into a bowl.
3. Add salt, pepper, and lemon juice to the avocado and mash with a fork until smooth.
4. Spread the mashed avocado evenly over each slice of toasted bread.
5. If desired, top each toast with a poached egg for additional protein.
6. Serve immediately while the toast is still warm.

Tip: To poach eggs, bring a pot of water to a gentle simmer, add a splash of vinegar, and slide in the eggs one at a time. Cook for 3-4 minutes or until the whites are set and the yolks are runny.

Cottage Cheese with Pineapple Chunks

Ingredients:

- 1 cup cottage cheese
- 1 cup fresh pineapple chunks (or canned in juice, drained)
- Optional: a sprinkle of cinnamon or nutmeg

Instructions:

1. In a serving bowl, place the cottage cheese.
2. Top with pineapple chunks, distributing them evenly over the cottage cheese.
3. For an extra touch of flavor, sprinkle with a pinch of cinnamon or nutmeg.
4. Serve chilled or at room temperature.

Tip: For a tropical twist, add a few tablespoons of shredded coconut or chopped nuts for extra texture.

Edamame with Sea Salt

Ingredients:

- 1 bag (about 12 oz) of frozen edamame in pods
- 1 teaspoon sea salt

Instructions:

1. Fill a large pot with water and bring it to a boil.
2. Add the frozen edamame to the boiling water and cook for about 5 minutes, or until the edamame is tender and heated through.
3. Drain the edamame and transfer it to a serving bowl.
4. Sprinkle with sea salt and toss to coat evenly.
5. Serve warm as a healthy and protein-rich snack.

Tip: For added flavor, toss the edamame with a dash of soy sauce or a sprinkle of chili flakes after cooking.

Peanut Butter and Banana Rice Cakes

Ingredients:

- 3 rice cakes
- 3 tablespoons natural peanut butter
- 1 large banana, sliced
- Optional: a sprinkle of cinnamon or a drizzle of honey

Instructions:

1. Evenly spread 1 tablespoon of natural peanut butter on each rice cake.
2. Top each rice cake with slices of banana, arranging them in a single layer.
3. For added sweetness, drizzle honey over the banana slices or sprinkle with cinnamon.
4. Serve immediately as a crunchy, **satisfying snack.**

Tip: For a nut-free alternative, use **sunflower seed butter** instead of peanut butter.

Cucumber Slices with Hummus

Ingredients:

- 1 large cucumber
- 1 cup hummus (store-bought or homemade)
- Optional: a sprinkle of paprika or sesame seeds

Instructions:

1. Wash the cucumber thoroughly and slice it into rounds about 1/4 inch thick.
2. Arrange the cucumber slices on a serving platter.
3. Serve with hummus on the side for dipping.
4. For extra flavor, sprinkle the hummus with paprika or sesame seeds before serving.

Tip: To make it more colorful, use a mix of cucumbers and other veggies like bell pepper strips or carrot sticks.

Turkey and Cheese Roll-Ups

Ingredients:

- 4 slices of deli turkey
- 4 slices of cheese (such as cheddar or Swiss)
- 1 whole-grain tortilla
- Optional: a handful of spinach or arugula leaves

Instructions:

1. Lay the tortilla flat on a clean surface.
2. Place the turkey slices evenly over the tortilla, followed by the cheese slices.
3. If using, lay spinach or arugula leaves over the cheese.
4. Roll the tortilla tightly, starting from one end, to form a log.
5. Slice the roll into bite-sized pieces, about 1 inch thick.
6. Secure each piece with a toothpick if needed and serve as a protein-rich snack.

Tip: Add a smear of mustard or mayonnaise before rolling for extra flavor.

Dark Chocolate and Almonds

Ingredients:

- 2-3 squares of dark chocolate (70% cocoa or higher)
- 1/4 cup raw or roasted almonds

Instructions:

1. Break the dark chocolate into small squares if not already done.
2. Arrange the chocolate squares and almonds on a small plate or in a bowl.
3. Enjoy by pairing each piece of chocolate with a few almonds.

Tip: For a more indulgent experience, melt the dark chocolate in the microwave in short bursts, stirring frequently, and dip the almonds in the melted chocolate. Allow them to cool on parchment paper before serving.

Apple Slices with Almond Butter

Ingredients:

- 1 large apple (such as Honeycrisp or Fuji)
- 3 tablespoons almond butter
- Optional: a sprinkle of cinnamon

Instructions:

1. Wash the apple thoroughly, then core and slice it into thin wedges.
2. Arrange the apple slices on a serving plate.
3. Serve the almond butter on the side for dipping.
4. For added flavor, sprinkle the apple slices with cinnamon before serving.

Tip: For a smooth consistency, slightly warm the almond butter in the microwave for 10-15 seconds before serving.

Roasted Chickpeas with Spices

Ingredients:

- 1 can (15 oz) chickpeas, drained and rinsed
- 1 tablespoon olive oil
- 1/2 teaspoon salt
- 1/2 teaspoon paprika
- 1/2 teaspoon garlic powder
- 1/4 teaspoon cayenne pepper (optional for heat)

Instructions:

1. Preheat your oven to 400°F (200°C).
2. Pat the chickpeas dry with paper towels to remove excess moisture.
3. In a mixing bowl, combine the chickpeas, olive oil, salt, paprika, garlic powder, and cayenne pepper (if using). Toss until the chickpeas are evenly coated.
4. Spread the chickpeas in a single layer on a baking sheet.
5. Roast in the oven for 25-30 minutes, stirring halfway through, until crispy and golden brown.
6. Let cool slightly before serving as a fiber-rich snack.

Tip: Store any leftover roasted chickpeas in an airtight container at room temperature to maintain their crunchiness.

Hard-Boiled Eggs with Paprika

Ingredients:

- 4 large eggs
- 1/2 teaspoon paprika
- Salt and pepper to taste

Instructions:

1. Place the eggs in a saucepan and cover with cold water by about an inch.
2. Bring the water to a boil over medium-high heat.
3. Once boiling, cover the saucepan and remove it from the heat. Let the eggs sit in the hot water for about 9-12 minutes, depending on your preferred level of doneness.
4. Drain the hot water and transfer the eggs to a bowl of ice water to cool for about 5 minutes.
5. Peel the eggs and slice them in half.
6. Sprinkle with paprika, salt, and pepper before serving.

Tip: For an extra flavor kick, try using smoked paprika or adding a dash of hot sauce.

Berry and Nut Yogurt Parfait

Ingredients:

- 1 cup Greek yogurt
- 1/2 cup mixed berries (such as blueberries, strawberries, or raspberries)
- 1/4 cup mixed nuts (such as almonds, walnuts, or pecans), chopped
- 1 tablespoon honey (optional)

Instructions:

1. In a glass or bowl, add a layer of Greek yogurt.
2. Top with a layer of mixed berries.
3. Add a layer of chopped nuts.
4. Repeat the layers until all ingredients are used, finishing with a sprinkle of nuts on top.
5. Drizzle with honey for added sweetness, if desired.

Tip: For a crunchy texture, add a layer of granola between the yogurt and berries.

Celery Sticks with Almond Butter

Ingredients:

- 4 large celery stalks
- 1/4 cup almond butter
- Optional: raisins or dried cranberries for topping

Instructions:

1. Wash the celery stalks thoroughly and cut them into 3-4 inch sticks.
2. Spread about 1 tablespoon of almond butter into the groove of each celery stick.
3. For a sweet touch, top with raisins or dried cranberries.
4. Serve immediately as a crunchy, healthy snack.

Tip: For variety, try using peanut butter or sunflower seed butter in place of almond butter.

Mini Caprese Skewers

Ingredients:

- 1 pint cherry tomatoes
- 1 package (8 oz) mozzarella balls (bocconcini or ciliegine)
- Fresh basil leaves
- Balsamic glaze
- Salt and pepper to taste
- Toothpicks or small skewers

Instructions:

1. Wash the cherry tomatoes and basil leaves thoroughly.
2. On each skewer or toothpick, thread one cherry tomato, one basil leaf, and one mozzarella ball.
3. Repeat the process until all ingredients are used.
4. Arrange the skewers on a serving platter.
5. Drizzle with balsamic glaze and season with salt and pepper.
6. Serve immediately as a refreshing and easy snack.

Tip: For added flavor, marinate the mozzarella balls in olive oil, garlic, and herbs for about 30 minutes before assembling the skewers.

Popcorn with Nutritional Yeast

Ingredients:

- 1/2 cup popcorn kernels
- 2 tablespoons coconut or olive oil
- 3 tablespoons nutritional yeast
- Salt to taste

Instructions:

1. In a large pot, warm the oil over medium-high heat.
2. Place a few popcorn kernels into the pot and secure it with a lid.
3. Once the initial kernels pop, add the remaining popcorn kernels and cover.
4. Gently shake the pot from time to time until the popping reduces to roughly one pop every few seconds.
5. Remove the pot from heat and transfer the popcorn to a large bowl.
6. Sprinkle the nutritional yeast and salt over the popcorn, tossing to coat evenly.
7. Serve immediately for a savory, cheesy-flavored snack.

Tip: For an extra kick, add a sprinkle of cayenne pepper or smoked paprika to the nutritional yeast mixture.

Quinoa Salad Cups

Ingredients:

- 1 cup of prepared quinoa
- 1/2 cup of cucumber, diced
- 1/2 cup of cherry tomatoes, cut in half
- 1/4 cup of red onion, finely chopped
- 1/4 cup of fresh parsley, chopped
- 2 tablespoons of olive oil
- 1 tablespoon of lemon juice
- Salt and pepper, to taste
- Small lettuce or endive leaves for serving

Instructions:

1. In a large bowl, combine the cooked quinoa, cucumber, cherry tomatoes, red onion, and parsley.
2. In a small bowl, combine the olive oil and lemon juice by whisking them together to create a dressing.
3. Drizzle the dressing over the quinoa mixture and toss until everything is evenly coated.
4. Add salt and pepper to suit your taste preferences.
5. Spoon the quinoa salad into individual lettuce or endive leaves for an easy finger food option.
6. Serve immediately or refrigerate until ready to serve for a flavorful and healthy appetizer.

Tip: Add crumbled feta cheese or chopped nuts for extra protein and texture.

Smoked Salmon on Rye Crackers

Ingredients:

- 12 rye crackers
- 4 oz cream cheese, softened
- 4 oz smoked salmon, sliced
- Fresh dill for garnish
- 1 lemon, cut into wedges

Instructions:

1. Spread about 1 teaspoon of cream cheese onto each rye cracker.
2. Top each cracker with a slice of smoked salmon.
3. Garnish with a small sprig of fresh dill.
4. Arrange on a platter and serve with lemon wedges for squeezing over the top.

Tip: For extra flavor, mix a bit of lemon zest into the cream cheese before spreading it on the crackers.

Sweet Potato Chips with Guacamole

Ingredients:

- 2 large sweet potatoes, sliced thinly
- 2 tablespoons of olive oil
- 1 teaspoon of salt
- 1/2 teaspoon of paprika
- 2 ripe avocados
- 1/4 cup of red onion, diced
- Juice of 1 lime
- 1/4 cup of cilantro, chopped
- Salt and pepper to your taste

Instructions:

1. Set your oven to 375°F (190°C) and allow it to preheat.
2. Toss the sweet potato slices with olive oil, salt, and paprika in a large bowl.
3. Arrange the slices in a single layer on a baking sheet.
4. Bake for 20-25 minutes, flipping halfway through, until the chips are crisp and golden brown.
5. For the guacamole, mash the avocados in a bowl and mix in red onion, lime juice, cilantro, salt, and pepper.
6. Serve the warm sweet potato chips with a side of guacamole.

Tip: Use a mandolin slicer for evenly thin sweet potato slices, ensuring uniform cooking.

Trail Mix with Dried Fruit and Seeds

Ingredients:

- 1 cup almonds
- 1 cup cashews
- 1/2 cup pumpkin seeds
- 1/2 cup sunflower seeds
- 1/2 cup dried cranberries
- 1/2 cup raisins
- 1/2 cup dark chocolate chips (optional)

Instructions:

1. In a large mixing bowl, combine almonds, cashews, pumpkin seeds, sunflower seeds, dried cranberries, and raisins.
2. If desired, add dark chocolate chips for a sweet touch.
3. Mix all ingredients thoroughly and store them in an airtight container.

Tip: Customize your trail mix by adding your favorite nuts and seeds or substituting dried cherries or apricots for the cranberries and raisins.

Carrot and Cucumber Sushi Rolls

Ingredients:

- 2 large carrots, peeled and julienned
- 1 cucumber, peeled and julienned
- 4 nori sheets
- 1/2 cup hummus
- Soy sauce or tamari for dipping
- Optional: sesame seeds for garnish

Instructions:

1. Lay a nori sheet on a clean, flat surface or sushi mat, shiny side down.
2. Spread a thin layer of hummus over the nori sheet, leaving about 1 inch at the top edge.
3. Arrange a few julienned carrot and cucumber slices horizontally across the nori sheet.
4. Starting from the bottom, tightly roll up the nori sheet, using the hummus-free edge to seal the roll.
5. Repeat with the remaining nori sheets and filling.
6. Slice each roll into bite-sized pieces.
7. Serve with soy sauce or tamari for dipping, and sprinkle with sesame seeds if desired.

Tip: For added flavor, include avocado slices or a sprinkle of pickled ginger in the rolls.

Protein Pancakes with Berries

Ingredients:

- 1 cup protein powder (vanilla-flavored works well)
- 1 cup oat flour or whole wheat flour
- 1 teaspoon baking powder
- 1 cup almond milk
- 1 egg
- 1 teaspoon vanilla extract
- 1 cup mixed fresh berries (such as blueberries, raspberries, or strawberries)

Instructions:

1. In a large bowl, mix the protein powder, flour, and baking powder.
2. In another bowl, whisk together the almond milk, egg, and vanilla extract.
3. Pour the wet ingredients into the dry ingredients and stir until just combined.
4. Warm a non-stick skillet on medium heat and lightly coat it with a bit of oil or cooking spray.
5. For each pancake, ladle 1/4 cup of batter onto the skillet.

6. Cook the batter until you see bubbles appear on the top, then flip it over and continue cooking until the other side turns golden brown.
7. Serve pancakes topped with fresh berries.

Tip: Make a big batch and store it in the fridge. Reheat individual pancakes in a toaster for a quick snack.

Chia Seed Pudding with Mango

Ingredients:

- 1/2 cup chia seeds
- 2 cups almond milk
- 1 tablespoon honey or maple syrup
- 1 teaspoon vanilla extract
- 1 ripe mango, diced

Instructions:

1. In a mixing bowl, combine chia seeds, almond milk, honey (or maple syrup), and vanilla extract.
2. Mix thoroughly to make sure the chia seeds are spread evenly.
3. Cover the mixture and place it in the refrigerator for a minimum of 4 hours or overnight, allowing it to thicken to a pudding-like texture.
4. Before serving, stir the pudding to break up any clumps.
5. Divide the pudding into serving bowls and top with diced mango.

Tip: For an extra tropical flavor, add shredded coconut or a sprinkle of nutmeg to the pudding before chilling.

Baked Kale Chips with Sea Salt

Ingredients:

- 1 bunch kale
- 1 tablespoon olive oil
- 1/2 teaspoon sea salt

Instructions:

1. Preheat your oven to 300°F (150°C).
2. Wash the kale thoroughly and dry it completely. Remove the stems and tear the leaves into bite-sized pieces.
3. In a big bowl, mix the kale pieces with olive oil and sea salt until they are thoroughly coated.
4. Arrange the kale pieces in one layer on a baking sheet.
5. Bake for 20-25 minutes, or until the edges are brown but not burnt, turning halfway through.
6. Let cool for a few minutes before serving as a crunchy, low-calorie snack.

Tip: Ensure the kale is completely dry before oiling to achieve maximum crispiness.

Zucchini Fries with Garlic Aioli

Ingredients:

- 2 medium-sized zucchinis
- 1 cup of breadcrumbs
- 1/2 cup of Parmesan cheese, grated
- 2 eggs, large
- 1 teaspoon of garlic powder
- Salt and pepper, as needed
- 1/2 cup of mayonnaise
- 2 minced garlic cloves
- 1 tablespoon of lemon juice

Instructions:

1. Preheat your oven to 425°F (220°C) and line a baking sheet with parchment paper.
2. Cut the zucchini into strips, resembling fries.
3. In a shallow dish, mix breadcrumbs, Parmesan cheese, garlic powder, salt, and pepper.
4. In a separate bowl, whisk the eggs.
5. Take each zucchini strip, immerse it in the egg mixture, and then cover it with breadcrumbs.
6. Arrange the breadcrumb-covered zucchini strips on the baking sheet you have prepared.
7. Bake for 20-25 minutes, or until golden and crispy, turning once.

8. Meanwhile, prepare the garlic aioli by mixing mayonnaise, minced garlic, and lemon juice in a small bowl.
9. Serve the zucchini fries hot with garlic aioli on the side.

Tip: For extra crispiness, broil the fries for the last 2 minutes of baking.

Pita Bread with Tzatziki Sauce

Ingredients:

- 4 whole wheat pita breads
- 1 cup Greek yogurt
- 1 cucumber, grated and squeezed to remove excess water
- 2 cloves garlic, minced
- 1 tablespoon olive oil
- 1 tablespoon lemon juice
- 1 tablespoon fresh dill, chopped
- Salt and pepper to taste

Instructions:

1. In a medium bowl, combine Greek yogurt, grated cucumber, minced garlic, olive oil, lemon juice, dill, salt, and pepper. Mix well to create the tzatziki sauce.
2. Chill the sauce in the refrigerator for at least 30 minutes to allow the flavors to meld.
3. Slice the pita bread into wedges or strips.
4. Serve the pita bread alongside the chilled tzatziki sauce for dipping.

Tip: For an extra burst of flavor, lightly toast the pita bread before serving.

Lentil Dip with Veggie Sticks

Ingredients:

- 1 cup cooked lentils
- 2 cloves garlic, minced
- 2 tablespoons olive oil
- 2 tablespoons lemon juice
- Salt and pepper to taste
- Assorted veggie sticks (carrots, celery, bell peppers)

Instructions:

1. In a food processor, combine cooked lentils, garlic, olive oil, and lemon juice. Blend until smooth.
2. Season with salt and pepper to taste.
3. Transfer the dip to a serving bowl.
4. Serve with assorted veggie sticks for dipping.

Tip: Add a pinch of cumin or smoked paprika for extra flavor.

Cheese and Cherry Tomato Bites

Ingredients:

- 1 pint cherry tomatoes
- 8 oz block of cheese (cheddar or mozzarella), cut into cubes
- Fresh basil leaves (optional)
- Toothpicks or small skewers

Instructions:

1. Skewer a cherry tomato, a basil leaf, and a cube of cheese onto each toothpick or skewer.
2. Arrange the skewers on a serving platter.
3. Serve immediately as a fresh, protein-rich snack.

Tip: Drizzle with balsamic glaze for added flavor.

Banana Oat Bars

Ingredients:

- 3 ripe bananas, mashed
- 2 cups rolled oats
- 1/2 cup nuts or seeds (optional)
- 1 teaspoon vanilla extract
- 1/2 teaspoon cinnamon

Instructions:

1. Warm the oven to 350°F (175°C) and line a baking tray with parchment paper.
2. In a large bowl, mix mashed bananas, oats, nuts or seeds, vanilla extract, and cinnamon until well combined.
3. Spread the mixture evenly in the prepared baking dish.
4. Bake for 20-25 minutes or until the edges are golden brown.
5. Let cool, then cut into bars.

Tip: Add dark chocolate chips or dried fruit for extra sweetness.

Egg Muffins with Spinach and Feta

Ingredients:

- Six large eggs
- One cup of chopped fresh spinach
- Half a cup of crumbled feta cheese
- Salt and pepper, as desired
- Cooking spray that prevents sticking

Instructions:

1. Set your oven to 375°F (190°C) and coat a muffin tin with non-stick cooking spray.
2. In a mixing bowl, whisk the eggs, spinach, and feta cheese together, then season with salt and pepper to your liking.
3. Distribute the egg mixture evenly into the muffin tin that has been prepared.
4. Bake for 20-25 minutes or until the egg muffins are set and slightly golden.
5. Allow to cool slightly before removing from the tin.

Tip: These muffins can be stored in the fridge and reheated for a quick snack.

Almond Butter and Chia Seed Toast

Ingredients:

- 2 slices whole-grain bread
- 2 tablespoons almond butter
- 1 tablespoon chia seeds
- Optional: sliced banana or berries for topping

Instructions:

1. Toast the bread slices to your desired crispness.
2. Spread 1 tablespoon of almond butter on each slice.
3. Sprinkle chia seeds evenly over the almond butter.
4. Top with sliced banana or berries if desired.

Tip: For added sweetness, drizzle a bit of honey or maple syrup over the top.

7-Day Sample Meal Plan

In this chapter, we will provide a sample 7-day meal plan that incorporates the healthy and delicious recipes discussed in this guide. This meal plan can serve as a guide for creating your own personalized meal plan that fits your individual needs and preferences.

Day 1

- Breakfast: Egg Muffins with Spinach and Feta
- AM Snack: Baked Kale Chips with Sea Salt
- Lunch: Grilled Chicken and Quinoa Salad
- PM Snack: Lentil Dip with Veggie Sticks
- Dinner: Zucchini Fries with Garlic Aioli

Day 2

- Breakfast: Banana Oat Bars
- AM Snack: Cheese and Cherry Tomato Bites
- Lunch: Smoked Salmon on Whole Wheat Pita
- PM Snack: Almond Butter and Chia Seed Toast
- Dinner: Quinoa and Black Bean Bowl

Day 3

- Breakfast: Greek Yogurt with Berries and Chia Seeds
- AM Snack: Trail Mix with Dried Fruit and Seeds
- Lunch: Lentil and Veggie Soup
- PM Snack: Carrot and Cucumber Sushi Rolls
- Dinner: Grilled Tofu Stir-Fry with Brown Rice

Day 4

- Breakfast: Whole Grain Toast with Avocado and Egg
- AM Snack: Pita Bread with Tzatziki Sauce
- Lunch: Turkey Wrap with Spinach and Hummus
- PM Snack: Banana Oat Bars
- Dinner: Baked Lentil and Veggie Casserole

Day 5

- Breakfast: Protein Pancakes with Berries
- AM Snack: Sweet Potato Chips with Guacamole
- Lunch: Chickpea and Avocado Salad
- PM Snack: Mini Caprese Skewers
- Dinner: Roasted Chicken with Quinoa and Asparagus

Day 6

- Breakfast: Chia Seed Pudding with Mango
- AM Snack: Baked Kale Chips with Sea Salt
- Lunch: Grilled Vegetable and Hummus Wrap
- PM Snack: Cheese and Cherry Tomato Bites

- Dinner: Beef Stir-Fry with Brown Rice

Day 7

- Breakfast: Scrambled Eggs with Spinach and Feta
- AM Snack: Lentil Dip with Veggie Sticks
- Lunch: Salmon Salad with Mixed Greens
- PM Snack: Almond Butter and Chia Seed Toast
- Dinner: Baked Cod with Steamed Broccoli

This meal plan incorporates a variety of high-protein and high-fiber foods, utilizing specific recipes from the list to ensure balanced nutrition throughout the week.

Conclusion

Thank you for taking the time to explore this comprehensive guide on high-protein and high-fiber foods. By reaching this point, you've armed yourself with valuable knowledge about how these nutrient-rich foods can transform your health and well-being. The journey to optimal health is a rewarding one, and incorporating these foods into your diet is a crucial step in the right direction.

High-protein and high-fiber foods offer numerous benefits that support a healthier lifestyle. Protein is essential for muscle repair, growth, and overall body function, while fiber promotes digestive health and helps you feel full longer, aiding in weight management. Together, they provide a powerful combination that enhances energy levels and maintains stable blood sugar levels, which can prevent energy crashes and support metabolic health.

We've delved into a variety of foods that are rich in protein and fiber, from lean meats and legumes to whole grains and fresh produce. By incorporating these foods into your daily meals, you not only meet your nutritional needs but also enjoy diverse flavors and textures that keep your meals exciting and satisfying.

The guide also introduced you to practical recipes that are both delicious and easy to prepare. These recipes demonstrate how simple it can be to integrate high-protein and high-fiber foods into your diet. Whether you start your day with overnight oats or enjoy a quinoa salad for lunch, each meal is an opportunity to nourish your body and fuel your activities.

Moreover, the 7-day meal plan provides a blueprint for balanced eating throughout the week. By following this plan, or customizing it to fit your preferences, you can maintain consistency in your diet and enjoy the benefits of sustained energy and overall well-being.

As you move forward, remember that creating a healthy lifestyle is a journey rather than a destination. Start small by introducing one or two new foods or recipes each week. Listen to your body, be patient with yourself, and celebrate your progress along the way. Every small step counts, and over time, these steps lead to significant changes.

Embrace the variety and abundance that high-protein and high-fiber foods offer. By making these foods a staple in your diet, you are investing in your health and setting the stage for a vibrant, energetic life. Stay committed to your goals, and enjoy the journey of discovering new tastes and healthier habits.

Thank you once again for being part of this guide. Your commitment to learning and improving your diet is commendable, and I hope the insights and tools provided here empower you to make informed, beneficial choices. Here's to your health and happiness, as you continue to explore the delicious world of high-protein and high-fiber foods. Keep nourishing your body with goodness, and let your newfound knowledge guide you to a healthier, more fulfilling lifestyle.

FAQs

What are the main benefits of incorporating high-protein and high-fiber foods into my diet?

High-protein and high-fiber foods help support muscle development, enhance digestion, provide sustained energy, and aid in weight management. They also promote overall health by maintaining stable blood sugar levels and supporting metabolic functions.

How can I start incorporating more high-protein and high-fiber foods into my meals?

Begin by assessing your current diet to identify gaps. Make simple swaps, such as using whole grains instead of refined grains, and add protein-rich foods like lean meats, legumes, or Greek yogurt into your meals. Gradually introduce new high-fiber fruits and vegetables to your diet.

Are there any quick and easy recipes for high-protein and high-fiber meals?

Yes, the guide includes 41 beginner-friendly recipes like overnight oats with chia seeds, quinoa and black bean salad, and grilled chicken wraps. These recipes are designed to be easy to prepare while incorporating nutrient-rich foods.

How do I create a balanced meal plan with high-protein and high-fiber foods?

Use the sample 7-day meal plan as a guide, which includes diverse meals and snacks throughout the day. Ensure each meal includes a good balance of protein and fiber to maintain energy levels and support digestive health.

Can I follow a high-protein and high-fiber diet if I am vegetarian or vegan?

Absolutely. Plant-based proteins such as tofu, tempeh, lentils, beans, nuts, and seeds are excellent sources of both protein and fiber. The guide provides recipes that can cater to vegetarian and vegan preferences while ensuring nutritional balance.

What are some common challenges when transitioning to a high-protein and high-fiber diet, and how can I overcome them?

Common challenges include adjusting to new foods and textures or experiencing digestive changes. Start slowly by introducing one or two new foods a week, and ensure you're drinking enough water to help your body adjust to increased fiber intake.

Can high-protein and high-fiber foods help with weight management?

Yes, they can. Protein helps boost metabolism and preserve lean muscle mass, while fiber increases feelings of fullness, reducing overall calorie intake. Together, they can create a dietary framework that supports healthy weight management.

References and Helpful Links

Smith, C., & Smith, C. (2024, February 3). Ultimate Guide to a High fiber, High protein Diet - A poised perspective. A Poised Perspective. https://apoisedperspective.com/ultimate-guide-to-a-high-fiber-high-protein-diet/

BSc, K. G. (2023, May 3). 22 high fiber foods you should eat. Healthline. https://www.healthline.com/nutrition/22-high-fiber-foods

Artyshchuk, O. (2022, March 30). Fiber and protein: Why a high protein high fiber diet will change your life - MyCHN Community Health Network. MyCHN Community Health Network. https://mychn.org/fiber-and-protein/#:~:text=A%20diet%20high%20in%20fiber,for%20a%20long%20healthy%20life.

Carle Illinois College of Medicine Office of Marketing and Communications. (n.d.). Weight-loss Success Depends on Eating More Protein, Fiber while Limiting Calories, Study Finds. Carle Illinois College of Medicine | Illinois. https://medicine.illinois.edu/news/weight-loss-success-depends-on-eating-more-protein-fiber-while-limiting-calories-study-finds#:~:text=%E2%80%9CThe%20research%20strongly%20suggests%20that,nutritionist%20for%20the%20iDip%20program.

BSc, K. G. (2023a, February 9). 10 Science-Backed reasons to Eat More Protein. Healthline. https://www.healthline.com/nutrition/10-reasons-to-eat-more-protein

Rd, B. L. K. M. (2024, October 2). 7-Day High-Protein, High-Fiber Anti-Inflammatory meal plan, created by a dietitian. EatingWell. https://www.eatingwell.com/7-day-high-protein-high-fiber-anti-inflammatory-meal-plan-8384508

Goggins, L. (2023, June 15). 32 High-Protein, High-Fiber dinner recipes. EatingWell. https://www.eatingwell.com/gallery/7952332/high-protein-high-fiber-dinner-recipes/

www.ingramcontent.com/pod-product-compliance
Lightning Source LLC
LaVergne TN
LVHW012029060526
838201LV00061B/4523